Appropriate Technology for Rural Development: The ITDG Experience

D.W.J.Miles

This paper was prepared for the Expert Meeting on New Modalities for the Actions of the Organisation in the Field of Technologies for Rural Development, co-ordinated by UNESCO, 7 Place de Fontenoy, 75700 Paris, France, in Brussels, 19-22 May 1980. It is reprinted here with their kind permission.

Practical Action Publishing Ltd
25 Albert Street, Rugby, CV21 2SD, Warwickshire, UK
www.practicalactionpublishing.com

© Intermediate Technology Publications 1982

First published 1982\Digitised 2013

ISBN 10: 1 85339 367 3
ISBN 13 Paperback: 9781853393679
ISBN Library Ebook: 9781780441665
Book DOI: https://doi.org/10.3362/9781780441665

All rights reserved. No part of this publication may be reprinted or reproduced or utilized in any form or by any electronic, mechanical, or other means, now known or hereafter invented, including photocopying and recording, or in any information storage or retrieval system, without the written permission of the publishers.

A catalogue record for this book is available from the British Library.

The authors, contributors and/or editors have asserted their rights under the Copyright Designs and Patents Act 1988 to be identified as authors of their respective contributions.

Since 1974, Practical Action Publishing has published and disseminated books and information in support of international development work throughout the world. Practical Action Publishing is a trading name of Practical Action Publishing Ltd (Company Reg. No. 01159018), the wholly owned publishing company of Practical Action. Practical Action Publishing trades only in support of its parent charity objectives and any profits are covenanted back to Practical Action (Charity Reg. No. 247257, Group VAT Registration No. 880 9924 76).

Reasonable efforts have been made to publish reliable data and information, but the author and publisher cannot assume responsibility for the validity of all materials or for the consequences of their use.

The manufacturer's authorised representative in the EU for product safety is Lightning Source France, 1 Av. Johannes Gutenberg, 78310 Maurepas, France.
compliance@lightningsource.fr

ORIGINS AND DEFINITIONS

By the end of the century, now less than twenty years away, the number of people of working age in the less developed countries (LDCs) will have increased from about 800 millions to about 1.3 billion. This is a fact, and nothing can be done to alter it. The extra 500 million people have either been born already or very soon will be. What we do not know is whether they will be working productively in a friendly environment or scratching a living in shanty towns or city slums.

There is still time to influence the outcome, providing policies, programmes and actions are intelligently directed towards solving the decisive problem of providing employment opportunities where they are needed and on a massive scale. These jobs will have to be made available where the people are – in the rural areas of developing countries. The number of jobs can only match the demand if the chosen technologies are appropriate.

At least there is now a general recognition that technology is a factor that must be subject to both discussion and choice. Technology is not neutral. It shapes the pattern of peoples' lives: what work they do and where and how they live. The introduction of a new technology will not benefit everybody equally – unless there are social, political and economic arrangements to offset the imbalance arising from it. Thus developing countries are increasingly coming to realise that the location of investment and the selection of technology present areas for critical choice. They are no longer prepared to take on a packaged foreign technology and apply it irrespective of local social and environmental conditions. It is recognised that technology is in fact an important (some would say, the most important) variable in development strategy.

This was far from being the general view when the Intermediate Technology Development Group Ltd. (ITDG) started its operations in 1965 and the change in opinion owes a good deal, we believe, to the Group's own activities over the past fifteen years. The concept of intermediate technology was formulated by the late Dr. E.F. Schumacher in a report prepared for the Indian Planning Commission in 1963 and subsequently presented in a paper to the Cambridge Conference on Rural Industrialisation in 1964. The basic argument that was the starting point for the Group was that the source and centre of world poverty lies primarily in the rural areas of poor countries. The only practical way to help these people is by introducing technologies that are cheap enough and simple enough to be used by rural and small-town populations without sophisticated technical and organisational skills, and with very low incomes. It was felt that unless poverty was tackled at its source, i.e. in the rural areas, outside the big cities, it would continue to manifest itself in three ways, mass migration into cities, mass unemployment and the persistent threat (or actuality) of mass starvation.

Before pursuing the argument further, it would be helpful to examine some possible definitions. Let us start with the word "technology" itself. Technology is the means by which we apply our understanding of the natural world to the solution of practical problems. It is a combination of 'hardware' (machines, tools and equipment) and 'software' (skills, knowledge, experience together with suitable organisational and institutional arrangements). All technological advances are the fruit of human ingenuity and resourcefulness. But if technology is to be useful, it is not sufficient for it to be available. It must also be applied and maintained, which implies a demand for a further input of a suitable range of human resources and skills. It is this latter input that is at the root of the difficulty in transferring technologies between differing environments. Technology hardly ever comes in a discrete electro-mechanical package with a single on-off switch that can be operated by anyone who can make use of a transistor radio. It is, or becomes, part of a complex system or process and makes its own demands. Thus a sophisticated technology in an unsophisticated environment can be transformed from a "good servant" to a "bad master" and distort – or even ultimately destroy – a previously stable, albeit imperfect, socio-economic pattern.

Technology can also be defined as 'human action on physical objects or as a set of physical objects characterised by serving human purposes'. Either way the realm and subject matter of the study of technology is human work. We are becoming aware that the major questions regarding technology are not technical but human questions, and are coming to understand that a knowledge of the history and evolution of technology is essential to an understanding of human history. Drucker rightly asks: "What does technology do to man as well as for him? For it is only too obvious that technology brings problems, disturbances and dangers as well as benefits."[1]   Now we have the noun "technology", but we need as adjective to limit and define it. There is no shortage of choice! Appropriate technology has become a part of the international language of development, and has generated a flood of articles, reports and papers devoted to the comparative semantic merits of "appropriate", "alternative", "adopted", "intermediate", "small-size", "low-capital", "self-reliant" and "soft" technologies. Amongst this plethora of terms, let us confine ourselves to differentiating between Appropriate Technology (AT) and Intermediate Technology (IT).

One workable definition of Appropriate Technology is "technology appropriate to a country's factors of production in that it maximises the use of factors which are locally plentiful and minimises the use of those which are locally scarce".[2] AT also, however, "represents what one might call the social and cultural dimension of innovation. The idea here is that the value of a new technology lies not only in its economic viability and its technical soundness, but in its adaptation to the local social and cultural environment. Assessing the appropriateness of a technology necessarily implies some sort of value judgement both on the part of those who develop it and those who will be using it."[3]

Because objectives and circumstances vary between (and within) countries and over time, the concept of appropriate technology is dynamic rather than static. It is not possible to award a "seal of approval" to any one technology as being universally appropriate to the provision of a given product or service. A technology can only be accepted as appropriate as a result of real or implicit choice among a range of possible alternatives, based on an objective evaluation of all aspects of their various impacts upon local conditions and requirements. For example, concrete blocks can be manufactured using a wide variety of techniques ranging from a simple manually-operated press to high-output capital-intensive specialised machinery. The simplest and cheapest solution would be likely to be most appropriate for occasional small-scale production in a remote village, while a more complex technology might be legitimately preferred by a contractor working on a large housing site on the outskirts of the capital city. This aspect of choice is reflected in a further definition of AT provided by the ILO: "A technology is appropriate if it is more suitable to actual local conditions and national social and economic objectives than any other technology resulting in a similar good or service."[4]

A final criterion by which the appropriateness of a technology may be judged is the degree of risk implied by the proposed strategy. A country may be persuaded by a financial cost-benefit analysis to import a single turn-key brick-making factory which would supply all its requirements. Such analyses can, but seldom do, take account of the disruption that will result if the facility fails to perform in line with expectations. Besides the social cost that will in any event result from displacing the many existing small brick-making (and concrete block-manufacturing) enterprises, the single source option would render the whole building materials and construction sector much more vulnerable to the effects of a single breakdown. The supply could be interrupted at source due to a failure resulting from inadequate maintenance procedures or delays in the delivery of imported spare parts. Even if the factory itself achieved planned levels of output, some parts of the country could suffer from irregular supplies if transport arrangements proved insufficient, perhaps due to the effect of generating additional traffic on an already inadequate road system. The alternative of setting up a programme to upgrade the multitude of small existing brick-makers may be more time-consuming and difficult to administer, but it would have the crucial merit of a "fail-safe" approach, as well as ensuring that the benefits of additional investment were widespread throughout the country. Deliberate risk avoidance and a preference for "fail-safe" solutions are therefore important factors which should be given due weight by those with responsibility for choosing which level of technology is most appropriate in a given case.

AT and IT are often treated as interchangeable, but there is a difference. As Dr. Schumacher, founder of ITDG, often said, AT really poses a series of questions "appropriate for what, to whom, etc."[5] The expression Intermediate Technology seeks to provide an answer for developing countries – namely that in most circumstances the most appropriate technologies are likely to be found among that range of technologies which lie between the subsistence technology of primitive societies and the highly sophisticated technology of industrial societies. Such intermediate technologies will be capital – and energy – saving, small-scale and employment generating, capable of being used locally so as to provide work where people live and relatively simple so that they can be made, operated and maintained by local people using local resources. In addition it is likely that they will be used primarily to produce goods and benefits for the local community.

Intermediate technologies are emphatically **NOT** second-best technologies. The IT practitioner does not operate in the simple one-dimensional world of the technician whose concern is limited to further advance along a well-trodden path. He has to accept the much more complex working environment of the real world in which the merits and risks of any proposed technology must be measured along the further two dimensions represented by human needs and human resources. For this effort only the best knowledge is good enough. Indeed, experience shows that it often needs a higher level of creativity to advance on the frontier of knowledge conducive to IT than is required in conventional research and development work. It is necessary to go back to first principles and to recognise constraints which exist in conditions of poverty and are absent in conditions of affluence. The road to the cheap and simple solution often demands the deployment of the most sophisticated thought processes and calculations, and can be successfully travelled only with the help of the latest and best research equipment.[5]

ITDG does not claim that an intermediate level of technology is necessarily the most appropriate for adoption in every case. In some industries, such as the petro-chemical industry, it is at present a fact that acceptable qualities and volumes of production can only be obtained in large manufacturing complexes, using sophisticated capital intensive techniques. We do, however, emphasise that the concept of appropriate technology is meaningless unless a choice of technologies is available from which the client or clients can select whichever appears most suitable to their own circumstances. At present a meaningful choice of technology is difficult to achieve due to the disequilibrium in availability of information between different types of technology. It is this knowledge gap, which ITDG originally identified (and seeks to bridge), which makes a rational choice between technologies so difficult. The labour-saving, capital-intensive, highly sophisticated technologies, designed for large-scale production in 'rich' markets and commonly used in the rich countries, are very well documented and easily accessible. But technologies applicable on a small scale by (or in) communities with plenty of labour and little capital, lacking technical and organisational sophistication are, on the whole, poorly documented, difficult to get hold of and, in many cases, even non-existent.

CHOICE OF TECHNOLOGY

It is basic to the whole purpose of the AT philosophy and approach that there should be a range of technologies available so that people can choose the one which is most appropriate to their particular circumstances and needs. Even when a wide range of technologies does exist, however, it is far from certain that the most appropriate one will be chosen and used in practice. In fact, instances of inappropriate choice of technology are all too frequent. To a large extent this happens because insufficient consideration is given to several important and inter-related issues: what are the prevailing conditions within which the choice is to be made; who makes the choice; and how is the choice to be made?

Prevailing Conditions

Since a technology can only be appropriate in terms of the particular circumstances in which it is to be used, it is obviously important to examine carefully what these circumstances are. Typically the key variables concern:

Labour: In general, developing countries have an abundance of very cheap but unskilled labour and, with exceptions like India and Egypt, a relative lack of technically trained and skilled craftsmen. Furthermore, labour is not simply another factor of production. As Dr. Schumacher pointed out 'development does not start with goods, it starts with people and their education, organisation and discipline'. [6] Therefore, the focus of good development programmes must start with labour. The fact that a large part of this labour is unemployed and underemployed in rural areas must also be borne in mind. In addition rural unemployment contributes to mass-migration to the cities, leading to a rate of urban growth which would tax the resources of even the richest societies and adding to the increase in urban unemployment. The focus of the labour situation is in the rural areas and what is needed is to maximise the work opportunities for the unemployed and underemployed.

Capital: A decade and a half ago, in the year that ITDG was formed, the UN World Economic Survey stated that 'All developing countries face a severe shortage of the capital necessary to begin and accelerate their development. Few of them even have sufficient resources to maintain a satisfactory rate of growth, say 5 per cent or greater, let alone being able to accelerate it'.[7]

In fact, in the words of the Economist of 19th August, 1978 the first law of economic growth has turned but to be biblical: to him who hath shall even more be given. According to the World Development Report (World Bank) the low-income countries saw their GNP per head grow by 0.9 per cent a year between 1960 and 1976, while middle income countries managed 2.8 per cent and industrialised countries had growth of 3.4 per cent. Since LDCs generally run current-account deficits, they have had to rely increasingly on capital inflows and, to make up for shortfalls on official aid, have turned increasingly to private finance. But higher levels of borrowing lead inevitably to more onerous debt servicing costs, and in this context alternative technologies that are less capital-hungry would appear to have increased attractions. Thus one of the main economic conditions prevailing in most LDCs is the shortage of capital, especially foreign exchange. In addition, in the rural areas there is often the additional problem that capital-intensive operations require high levels of infrastructure spending on roads, power supplies, etc., which can further deplete scarce capital resources.

Markets: Local markets for products of all kinds in rural areas tend to be restricted in size whether by virtue of the low per capita incomes, difficulties of transportation and high fuel costs. Thus the typical appeal of economies of scale may well be offset by the limitations to the market and the competitive position of smaller-scaled operations thereby enhanced. In some instances the size of markets is so limited where population is widely dispersed that even small-scale production itself becomes uneconomic and the need can be met only by centralised production and multi-goods distribution.

Similar difficulties arise with the supply system. The raw materials used by dispersed rural producers are expensive because of transport difficulties, the small size of their orders and the high cost of energy.

Resources: Aside from the basic importance of human resources to the development process, consideration should also be given to fuller utilisation of the physical resources available to LDCs. For both economic and social reasons, local self-sufficiency and independence need to be integrated into technological change. Indigenous resources, on balance, are likely to be better understood and controlled by local workers and they are more easily absorbed by the local culture.

Some of these parameters are at least partially identified when conventional financial appraisal techniques are employed, but these techniques are not designed to give full weight to those aspects which do not show up as costs or returns in direct monetary units. In countries where capital is scarce and labour either unemployed or underemployed, appraisal techniques should be deliberately geared so that they favour schemes which maximise capital productivity, simply because it is capital rather than labour which is in short supply. This approach would mean that priority would be given to products and processes which need the least capital input for any given value of output.

In theory the calculated and forecast unit costs on projected schemes would take account of the readier availability of labour (through lower projected wage costs) and lack of capital (through higher interest rates). In fact, perceived costs seldom reflect the real levels of availability accurately. Wage rates, although they may be low, are not related to the fact that there are large numbers of unemployed seeking work and may be kept up by some form of minimum wage law. Perceived interest rates also distort the equation, since they are often fixed artificially low as an act of policy and rarely reflect the scarcity of capital and the risk involved in financing a new technology in an environment for which it was not designed. The tendency of some countries to overvalue their currencies and ration foreign exchange allocations means that projects which demand heavy foreign exchange components appear paradoxically attractive since the foreign exchange would be converted at a much less favourable rate if the currency was valued at a free market rate.

It seems likely that a fairer reflection of the advantages of alternative technologies would be seen if some form of social cost benefit analysis based on shadow prices was to be employed, although it must be admitted that the estimation of shadow prices and of the social rate of discount is a fairly complex matter. Furthermore, it is also true that the data needed for the estimation of shadow prices and of the social rate of discount is a fairly complex matter. Furthermore, it is also true that the data needed for the estimation of shadow prices are often not available.

Who is to Choose and How?

At present it is probably fair to state that most technological choice is made by politicians, administrators, managers and engineers. Of all these groups, engineers might appear to be the best placed since they will have a technical background and should therefore be well able to make a critical examination of competing claims.

However, the author (an engineer himself) believes that the

selection of technology is too important to be left solely in the hands of professional engineers and technologists. Indeed the single-discipline training and lack of opportunity for inter-disciplinary project work, which still characterises the crucial early experience of so many of them, may lead to a tendency to believe that all problems must be solved by applying only known and conventional technologies.

Politicians, administrators and managers also tend to choose conventional technologies for various reasons including risk avoidance, appearance of modernity, lack of trained supervisory personnel and inappropriate incentive and reward systems.

If the technology chosen for a particular process is to be truly appropriate, it must be fully understood and accepted by those who are to install, operate and maintain it. The rural areas of developing countries are littered with the remains of promising projects imposed from above by those with – usually – the best interest of local people in mind. But imposed technologies seldom take root, since the responsibility for achieving objectives is not transferred from the decision-takers to those who are in a position to make the project work. Objectives are most likely to be accepted where the people concerned have contributed to making the original choice. Despite their poverty, rural communities usually have the key organisational advantage of being ready-made defined social units with their own loyalties and common goals. The aim should be to mobilise these group loyalties at the decision-making stage, and so enable the beneficiaries to acquire greater control over their own lives.

The aim of enfranchising these beneficiaries and so enabling them to achieve a greater degree of control over their lives is clearly more likely to be achieved with simpler technologies which will fit more easily into existing social and work patterns. They will then feel that they have a real autonomous responsibility for the necessary internal decision-making and control, and that there is a clear 'boundary' between the local system and the larger system (ministry, agency, etc.) of which it is effectively a part. The external agency which promotes the new technology will be more likely to achieve its own objectives by consciously 'drawing back' and concentrating on regulating the 'boundary conditions' which define its inter-action with the local system than by attempting to impose detailed control. The primary task is to provide the conditions within which the local group can achieve greater control both over its local physical environment and also in its transactions with its external social, economic and political environment. Unless there is a change in the relatedness of the local group to the wider system, no significant internal changes will be sustainable.

This is not to suggest that it is sufficient to make funds (and a list of promising alternative technologies) available to a village and give them carte blanche in spending it. It is more realistic to envisage a process of negotiation between the local group and the appropriate governmental development agency, assisted hopefully by a friendly representative from the nearest appropriate technology centre. In this way, local demands can be reconciled with regional and national priorities, which in turn will be modified by the pattern of local needs and aspitations that are expressed. Moreover, negotiation of development plans with the government agency will itself help the local community to organise itself, to learn to manage transactions across its boundary with the wider society and thereby enhance its own confidence and motivation.

The negotiation should be guided by people who are sensitive to the local and regional economic and social environment. Since the introduction of the new technology will affect this environment and the linkages between social, economic and technological parameters are always complex and usually very difficult to predict. It must be remembered that the transfer of technology, when properly administered, integrates a number of complementary activities; it provides for change in social systems and attitudes, it generates new knowledge and human skills; and it requires a fresh physical environment for its successful operation.

Aside from broadening the decision-making base to include local participation, it has also been argued that other improvements are needed. The selection of the most appropriate technology in any given instance is - providing it is properly done - by no means routine, and the analytical tools at present available to guide the process of evaluation and choice are imperfect (and sometimes even downright misleading). If this argument is accepted, it follows that there should be a definite effort to improve the quality of professional performance at the stage of decision making on the most preferable of a group of competing technologies. It is, therefore, encouraging that the ILO Management Development Branch is at present conducting a (limited) programme of research through national management development centres to determine:

- What are the characteristics and consequences of technological choices currently being made?
- How can the number and harmfulness of wrong choices be reduced?

It is envisaged that this research will lead on to the formulation of programmes for training managers in the process of appropriate technological choice. It will be a useful advance if the issue of training in technological choice becomes explicit rather than implicit in the curricula of technical and management training institutions. For in many developing countries there is already a hidden bias in the nature of the training provided by these institutions. Courses that teach sophisticated planning, control and preventive maintenance techniques prepare the students to design and operate technically-sophisticated plant and processes. On the other hand, an emphasis on supervisory training courses increases the number of workers – both industrial and clerical – who can be effectively supervised. A crucial constraint on the adoption of labour-intensive technologies (and a spur to mechanisation) is the difficulty of recruiting responsible and competent supervisory staff who will ensure that large gangs of human workers achieve the predicted levels of output that will enable them to compete favourably with a single machine. An industrial example is the need for many more construction foremen and charge-hands if roads are to be built and maintained using labour-based technologies. A non-industrial example is the attraction of computers and advanced office equipment being very limited if there is a good supply of well trained supervisors, clerks, secretaries and typists, backed up by a ready access to organisation and methods expertise. Training curricula, like technology itself, are never neutral, and countries and development institutions that are genuinely committed to promoting technologies that are appropriate should note that attitudes are linked to knowledge and skills, and are consequently often formed in the classroom, lecture hall, workshop and laboratory.

TECHNOLOGY DEVELOPMENT AND APPLICATION

Although the mechanisms for technology transfer and technology choice are in need of considerable improvement in most developing countries, this improvement alone will not be sufficient to ensure that overall development objectives are achieved. Firstly a new range of intermediate technologies must be developed to the 'packaged' stage where they can compete in ease of adoption and application with the more sophisticated technologies that are usually actively promoted by large enterprises backed by substantial financial, technical and marketing resources. In some ways the development of technology is easier than ensuring that it is disseminated and applied. That is the managerial stage in the process, and management should be above all, about 'getting things done'. It is not enough just to provide the hardware. Equal attention should be directed to improving organisational and institutional systems so that the hardware is effectively used.

It is now fashionable for every country to refer to its commitment to appropriate technology in its Development Plan. This mention of AT is, however, too often no more than a last minute gloss, giving the illusion of commitment but not backed up by motivation and coherent thought. What are needed are comprehensive national technology policies corresponding to the overall socio-economic development strategy of the countries concerned to guide decision-makers in their choice of technology, help to formulate supportive legal and financial programmes and make provision for the proper allocation of resources for training, research, development and eventual application.

Even in countries that do have some form of national science and technology policy – backed by related research institutions – the emphasis is usually on the "pure" R & D aspects rather than the "applied" social and commercial aspects that are vital to successful implementation. They are seldom directly related to corresponding national socio-economic policies and programmes and do not address themselves to the fiscal and other measures which are necessary before identified technologies can be translated into commercially-viable production processes. Too often they disregard the fact that although critical, ttechnology is in the end merely a tool to be used in the industrial process.

It has been suggested [8] that a national technology policy should aim at the implementation of the following procedures:

- Establish the basis for industrial development to conform with national political, social and economic objectives. This will identify and distinguish between those industries to be developed centrally, on a large scale, and those which are to be developed as small local enterprises.

- Establish central planning control procedures to give effect to the above and to ensure that the needs of the small industry sectors are adequately recognised and its products protected from foreign or large industry competition (through taxation, import licensing, etc.).

- In the case of large and medium scale industries, establish procedures to examine the feasibility of introducing simpler, more labour-intensive production processes.

- Examine the extent to which small service and processing industries can be generated in support of developments in large- and medium- scale operations.

- Make an equitable allocation of capital resources (finance and manpower) and share of capital investment (goods and services) between industrial sectors and between large-, medium- and small-scale needs.

- Review the provision of manpower training and extension services to ensure that they adequately reflect the needs of the different sectors – particularly in regard to small industry.

- Provide for and co-ordinate R & D facilities and institutions which are required to adapt or design, introduce and promote appropriate technologies.

- Establish procedures for introducing technology development programmes to test and evaluate the effectiveness of new technologies through pilot projects.

- Establish appropriate facilities to encourage successful projects and to promote them beyond the pilot project stage (credit, raw materials supplies, government bulk purchasing schemes, etc.).

— Create educational and other social programmes designed to help people recognise opportunities for industrial development, and provide them with the skills and incentives to take advantage of them.

The central problem of finding and applying appropriate technologies for development can be eased considerably by setting up some form of appropriate technology centre in the country concerned. ITDG has itself been instrumental in assisting in the setting up of a number of centres at national, or in some cases even at regional level. The function of such centres should be to develop local awareness and a local ability to solve technical problems, so that each centre will act as a focal point for the mobilisation of data on appropriate technologies and for their widespread dissemination.

Objectives of individual centres will depend to some extent upon national policies and priorities. One example is provided by the objectives of field projects set up by the Tanzania Small Industries Development Organisation[9]:

— To relate to one or other of the basic requirements for food, clothing, shelter or community needs;

— Their participants can genuinely gain a living out of the production process;

— The technology applied can be sustained with the local skills and resources;

— The materials and methods used and the market features can be readily comprehended by and are accessible to the local people;

— The scale of production and technology involve a low capital cost per workplace and are suitable for widespread dissemination throughout Tanzania.

Since it is an essential prerequisite for success that the people themselves should participate in the process, this consideration should also be reflected in the objectives of national AT programmes. The approved scheme of the Pakistan Appropriate Technology Development Programme in 1977 was "to motivate and inspire the people to undertake their own economic and social development by doing the planning themselves and executing such plans directly." [11] Stating that putting men and materials together does not automatically result in development, the scheme emphasises that it requires an inner urge to develop, which comes by motivating the people. The approved scheme comments that unless the people are motivated to undertake development for themselves it cannot be a self-growing process. The outside agency, according to the scheme, can only provide ingredients to quicken the process, like fertiliser acting in plant growth.

The location of a national centre for appropriate technologies can be varied according to the needs and opportunities present. Some existing centres are closely linked with governmental departments, others are non-governmental and voluntary in nature, and still others are based with academic research institutions. There are arguments that being based within a governmental agency such as the Ministry of Finance will ensure that recommendations of the centre and its programmes will be more likely to gain the co-operation of other governmental offices as well as possibly helping to generate additional programmes such as more favourable taxation, credit, trade regulations, etc. to support the new AT activities. Another potential location within the government would be to place an AT unit within the planning agency with the mandate to vet all planning and policy making from the point of view of its technological appropriateness and consistency with other AT goals and programmes. Alternatively, AT centres outside the orbit of governmental rules and regulations may find it easier to produce non-conventional technologies and to collaborate more closely and effectively with the wide range of non-governmental programmes often found at the grassroots levels. Finally, centres located at academic-research institutions may benefit from having greater outreach and impact within the country or community by virtue of their training facilities, extension workers, etc. and the resources for longer term R & D may be more readily available to them. Some national governments may lack the staff or other capacities to operate a successful AT centre. In other instances, direct governmental involvement may effectively preclude tapping the useful voluntary workers and their links with local needs and resources. There can be no hard and fast rule as to the best place to locate a new AT centre or how it should operate. However, our experience indicates that AT work should operate at the national level or below if it is to be effective in meeting local, rural needs and problems.

It is true that recent trends have tended to favour the establishment of regional AT institutions on the grounds that it is argued that local AT centres will have too few resources to be able to carry out serious work; that there is a danger of duplication and that where successful work takes place the results will not be disseminated to other countries. Although there is some superficial substance to these arguments, it is much more likely that the proposed regional institutions will prove bureaucratic rather than innovative with the result that they will have little positive impact upon the programmes of national governments or the lives of ordinary people. Further, such institutions will tend to draw away from national centres the more able (and scarce) practitioners by virtue of higher salaries, status and other inducements; thereby creating still greater problems for national efforts and often dealing only with the broader, more commonly shared needs rather than some severe but highly localised needs within a country. The whole AT concept, with its emphasis on the use of local resources by local people to serve local needs, runs counter to this tendency towards regionalisation.

It is accepted that unnecessary duplication should be avoided and there will obviously be instances where local resources and facilities will be insufficient to cope with specialised demands. But these potential disadvantages can be overcome by strengthening linkages between the separate national centres and making arrangements whereby existing research institutions at home or abroad respond to requests for help on a project specific basis. All these linkages will depend upon the flow of information to, between and through national AT centres. Thus the design of communication systems should be the subject of detailed attention. This does not necessarily mean that the answer lies in some form of all-embracing international AT data bank, since centralised mechanically-controlled systems tend to be over-rigid and undiscerning. ITDG's experience in handling technical enquiries suggests that a quick, thoughtful and brief response to a specific query is appreciated much more than a standardised (albeit very detailed) response which lacks the 'human touch'.

What we believe is needed is knowledge of knowledge – knowledge of who is doing what, and where and in what circumstances. This dynamic and flexible approach allows for the latest information to be drawn together from time to time and for specific purposes – either for periodic publication or in response to specific enquiries. Those who strive to provide information services, therefore, should seek to strengthen communications between the resource centres – of research and development, professional institutions and the like – manufacturers and industrialists already producing or involved in the use of appropriate technologies and prospective or involved in the use of appropriate technologies and prospective new clients of those technologies. Since ITDG sees itself as essentially a 'knowledge of knowledge organisation', that is perhaps an appropriate note on which to move on to an analysis of ITDG's experience during its first fifteen years and to assess its role and resources as an initiating and support insitution.

THE ITDG EXPERIENCE

The Intermediate Technology Development Group Ltd. was set up in 1965 as a non-profit company limited by guarantee, with the status of a registered charity. It had two parallel, but complementary, aims :
- To stimulate new thinking and action on the part of both rich and poor countries so that overseas development finance can work more effectively for the benefit of the whole community to which it is directed.
- To supply basic and applied research in the UK and training facilities on the spot to provide the type of industry best calculated to relieve unemployment and poverty in the developing countries.

From the start, the Group aimed not merely to supplement the existing aid programmes, but to change their emphasis; to change them away from treating poor countries as if they were rich countries in disguise, towards recognising that their problems are individual and often deep-seated, and above all towards recognising and acting upon their need to develop methods of self-help and self-reliance.

In the first of these aims - to gain acceptance for the concept of promoting and applying technologies that are appropriate to local needs - there can be no doubt that ITDG has had a remarkable impact. Before 1965, there were few if any organisations specifically committed to the development of practical alternatives for ordinary people. Now, there are hundreds of organisations committed, wholly or in part, to developing intermediate technologies. It has become a mark of respectability for national development plans to refer to a commitment to ensure that technologies employed within their frontiers are appropriate and most bilateral and international agencies are busy setting up AT units and programmes. This acceptance of the concept is of course encouraging. But a change of attitude alone is not enough, for the real test of an idea comes when it is translated into practical application. In the words of Jequier[11]:

- "Appropriate technology is here to stay, but it should also be realised that the scope and number of successful innovations in appropriate technology is for the moment still too limited to serve as a convincing and viable alternative to the types of technology we have to-day. The situation is somewhat similar to that of the automobile in 1890: this new technology looked to-day. The situation is somewhat similar to that of the automobile in 1890: this new technology looked very promising, particularly to those who had developed it, but it was not yet a competitive substitute to the railway and the horse-drawn carriage."

The second aim was perhaps even more ambitious than the first, for the Group commenced operations in an untried field, with scant resources and no clear structure or definition of individual responsibilities. In the early years it relied heavily on volunteer members of specialist advisory panels for technical guidance and replies to a growing stream of technical enquiries. The panel members, mainly professionally-qualified people with wide overseas experience, played a crucial role in demonstrating the potential of the Group and so enabling it to attract the funds that would finance the employment of full-time project staff.

By 1973, the year in which "Small is Beautiful" was published, the Group had begun to learn from the outcome of its early efforts and its activities were starting to yield tangible results. An Industrial Liaison Unit had been formed to answer the wide variety of requests for specific information on small-scale manufacturing techniques, and research and development units were working in the fields of agriculture, water, power, building and building materials. Although still small, ITDG was anxious to decentralise wherever possible and three subsidiary companies were formed to deal with aspects of the Group's work that could operate autonomously. The first (now IT Consultants Ltd.) arose from the experience gained in overseas visits and projects and the consequent demand for the Group to supply expertise on a commercial consultancy basis. Another subsidiary, Development Techniques Ltd., was formed to develop low cost technology 'hardware' for commercial production, following the successful development of a low-cost, limited output paper pulp packing machine. A growing publications programme covering training material, manuals and technical specifications, together with the new quarterly journal "Appropriate Technology", justified the creation of a third subsidiary (IT Publications Ltd.) to handle all Group publications.

In addition to its own direct activities, the Group has sought to assist and co-operate with a growing "network" of AT centres evolving in developing countries in Africa, Asia and Latin America. These include the Appropriate Technology Development Association, Lucknow, India, the Technology Consultancy Centre, Kumasi, Ghana and the South Pacific Appropriate Technology Foundation, Papua New Guinea. To help further the development of the "network" in Africa, two ITDG staff members were seconded to the Economic Commission for Africa for several years.

At this stage the aims of the Group were redefined and restated as follows[12]:

- To compile inventories of existing technologies which are used, or might be used by developing countries, within the concept of low-cost, labour-intensive production.

- To identify gaps in the range of technologies and the production opportunities which could be created if these gaps were filled.

- To research and develop new or more appropriate processes, by invention or modification.

- To test and demonstrate the use of intermediate technologies in the field and to advise and assist governments and organisations on their adoption.

- To make known the results of its work as widely as possible, by publications and other means, so as to facilitate the transfer and use of intermediate technologies in appropriate circumstances.

In 1978, the professional resources of ITDG were significantly strengthened with the creation of Intermediate Technology Industrial Services (IT-IS) as a new unit to replace the previous industrial liaison unit. IT-IS was set up with funds allocated by the British Ministry of Overseas Development and, thanks to the parallel financing of an Appropriate Technology Project Fund to be administered by the new unit, ITDG was for the first time able to provide financial as well as technical assistance to meet the needs of developing countries for unfamiliar or new technologies primarily in the small-scale industry sector.

The functions of IT-IS include responding to technical enquiries from developing countries and advising on the availability of existing intermediate technology products and processes; commissioning economic and technical studies to define the requirements for such technologies; organising the development, adaptation, testing and demonstration of such technologies; advising firms and agencies exporting or importing intermediate technical products and equipment. The AT Project Fund supports the development of new technologies including field testing; pilot demonstrations; establishment of pilot industrial projects; studies, market surveys and field visits related to the above; and projects designed to gather and disseminate information, through publications or by other means, on intermediate technology products and processes and their use.[13] IT-IS employs a group of Industrial Advisers who specialise by both field of technology and geographical area, and provide a first point of contact for all enquiries and requests for assistance. Each Adviser is responsible for a specific group of countries to which he makes regular visits to establish direct contact with those requiring the services of the unit. The Advisers also are responsible for defining the need for any new technologies, especially those of common interest to several countries.

The most recent development in ITDG's history has been the creation of two additional subsidiary companies: Intermediate Technology Transport Ltd. and Intermediate Technology Power Ltd. The main purpose of both of these subsidiaries is to provide professional advice and assistance in the assessment, development and implementation of appropriate policies and technologies for developing countries.

Whilst ITDG has always recognised that the ultimate measure of the value of the AT/IT idea must be the extent to which it results in a positive and beneficial change in the patterns of life in the 2 million villages of the developing world, as a still relatively small organisation we have to be reaistic about the direct impact we can achieve with our limited resources. Consequently we have focussed increasing attention on the boundaries between our own operations, those of the much larger and more powerful international and bilateral aid agencies, the governments of countries which we seek to help and the interests of our ultimate clients - the people who live in the poor rural communities of the developing countries.

In the late '60s and early '70s the Group's prime concern was to create a track record and test out its ideas and gain practical operating experience, and to this end it established a number of field projects overseas staffed by project officers employed by the Group. As the experience and standing of the Group grew, it became clear that further developments in the direction of becoming yet another field project agency would result in an unhelpful diversion of our resources from ITDG's unique role as a 'knowledge of knowledge' organisation. By defining and limiting our operational boundaries in this way, we could make a much more positive impact by providing technical advice and services to much larger agencies and governments engaged in field projects and programmes. Equally important, we could assist as a catalyst in the formation of local indigenous IT centres that would be better placed (thanks to their familiarity with local social, political and economic conditions) to deliver technologies that are tailor-made to the requirements of our ultimate clients - the rural poor.

The advantages of providing information, and developing appropriate technologies as close as possible to, the point of need had already been recognised. In 1970, UNIDO commissioned ITDG to investigate the establishment and operation of a technology service in Ghana based on the Kumasi University of Science and Technology. As a result, a Technology Consultancy Centre (TCC) was established on the University campus to provide information and advice to local entrepreneurs, undertake technology development and co-ordinate production initiatives. In the face of considerable difficulties, the TCC has been successful in stimulating the formation of a diverse clutch of small enterprises comprising glue and soap manufacture, the production of animal food from brewers' spent grain, broadloom weaving, glass beads, brass casting and metal work, nuts and bolts, and a plant construction unit (making storage tanks, tools and simple equipment). As one of the first national appropriate technology centres demonstrating that "small is possible as well as beautiful", the record of the TCC is of considerable general interest. For this reason ITDG recently commissioned the services of Ms Sally Holtermann, an independent economist, to make a detailed study of the TCC, including case studies of each of the eight component small enterprises.[14]

Since the establishment of the TCC, an increasing number of AT and IT centres have been created in developing countries, often with advice and assistance from ITDG. We hope and believe that links between ITDG and local IT centres will be further strengthened, and we are giving increasing consideration to the types of institutions and other measures required to translate isolated appropriate technology projects into commonly adopted national programmes. But suitable national policies are a prerequisite to the formation of national programmes, so ITDG is currently examing ways of analysing and evaluating policy measures affecting the dissemination, transfer and adoption of technology. In recent years, several countries (for example India, Kenya and Thailand) have introduced a variety of explicit policies aimed at encouraging the widespread introduction and use of appropriate technologies and the growth of small-scale decentralised industries. Other countries have introduced policies less explicitly geared to the encouragement of AT, but which are likely **inter alia** to favour it. Examples are the provision of credit to small farmers and entrepreveurs; setting up of technical assistance centres and extension schemes in rural areas; industrial licensing schemes favouring small businessmen; subsidies and other incentives such as preference in public sector purchasing arrangements. Preliminary research is now underway on this topic, with a view to identifying which current policy measures have proved most effective, thus enabling the Group to offer informed advice to agencies and national governments on the likely advantages and disadvantages of various forms of legislation and general policy measures.

IT Consultants Ltd., the Group's consultancy arm, plays an important role in the overall strategy of supplying expertise when, where and in the particular form that it is needed. Consultants on AT projects should obviously start with the requisite specialist technical knowledge but, more critically, should understand the nature and objectives of AT and also be flexible enough to be sensitive to the prevailing economic, social and political climate. If a local consultant is available to carry out the assignment this is generally advantageous, but in many developing countries the consulting profession is quite young and most of the available expertise is concentrated in government and direct administration, management and research.

A UNIDO Regional Workshop on the Use of Consultants focussed attention on the need for consultants to not only act as problem solvers but also as diagnosticians of related problems. It was suggested that, when consulting with national bodies concerned with national development plans, consultants should take into consideration the project's overall contribution to the country's economy and thus be willing to train local counterparts to deal with the after-service of such projects. [15] As a corollary one might comment that the client would be wise to assign properly qualified counterparts if full value is to be obtained from the assignment.

It should also be noted that most AT consultancy is related to small enterprises, and consultants therefore face a number of additional constraints that do not apply to larger organisations.[16] Some of them are :

> whereas large, well-organised enterprises can afford both good line management and specialist staff, the small enterprise manager is more isolated;

- the small enterprise manager often operates with inadequate or, at best, minimum quantative data;

- because small enterprises offer lower wages and fringe benefits with relatively poor job security and opportunities for promotion, there is difficulty in recruiting high calibre employees;

- difficulties in raising capital, particularly in financial crises;

- limited financial reserves and low borrowing capacity;

- although ability to change and adapt is a natural strength of the small enterprise this may be nullified if the manager is too occupied with on-going operational problems;

- difficulties in maximising human resources through staff training and development;

- the manager is not often able to understand and interpret government regulations, actions, concessions, etc. to his best advantage.

The consultant must be able to cope with these constraints, and should be interested in the distribution and method of output. He must recognise that the deliberate choice of high-employment, low-output technologies may in some circumstances be appropriate. He must also recognise and present the range of 'technology mixes' and investment strategies that is possible in any given situation.[17]

He must also recognise that, for smaller scale manufacturing enterprises, problems of technology cannot be separated from problems of management. Specific techniques for better management, conceived in relation to the abilities and circumstances of small businessmen, are not usually thought of as appropriate technology, but the problem of disseminating such ideas is basically the same as when physical goods or processes are involved. It is, in a sense, a problem of developing an appropriate diffusion system to match the nature and circumstances of the target audience. A new method of management, or manufacture is of no value unless it is taken to those whom it is intended to benefit; but they must not only become aware of the existence of the new idea, they must be helped to understand its value in relation to their own individual circumstances.[18]

In the past, the Group has engaged in ad hoc participation in courses mounted by academic institutions and occasional lectures and presentations by Group staff in the UK and overseas. More recently it has begun specialised project work on the training of small building contractors and on-the-job training in relation to project oriented developments. These aspects of communicating our ideas and experience are now likely to be given greater emphasis. We see serious "training gaps" at four levels :

> at the artisanal level, we see a need for practical training for people who will be using appropriate technologies, such as brick-makers, fabricators and installers of fibre-reinforced roof sheets, etc.,

> at the enabling level of supervisors, foremen and managers of labour-intensive operations in both the private and the public sectors, where a shortage of these front-line managers is often the critical constraint on the adoption of labour-based technologies since they can only be economically justified if the operators achieve acceptable levels of productivity;

> — at the professional level, where the Group will examine ways of presenting AT concepts and practical techniques for designers and operating staff of institutions and enterprises engaged on general development programmes and projects in the Third World; and

> at the political level, where planners, administrators and decision-makers need exposure to the wide variety of governmental and institutional changes which may support and make more effective implementation and expansion of AT programmes.

Development and expansion of on-the-job training efforts is basic to filling some of those gaps. Also practical training in planning, supervision, record-keeping, control and simple man-management techniques could make AT a much more practical proposition by raising levels of output to a more competitive level. ITDG has already gained considerable experience of basic small enterprise management training both for general business [19] and more specifically for the construction industry, resulting in the publication of three books aimed at helping small building contractors in developing countries to get themselves established and to run their businesses effectively. [20, 21, 22]. Greater efforts must also be made to reach professional and political levels through closer links between academic and research institutions and the practical field work in AT, as well as through initial efforts to delineate and articulate more clearly the characteristics of useful AT support programmes and methods for increasing them.

There is a further facet of the work of the Group which deserves mention. Although it was established primarily to assist developing countries in the choice of technologies best suited to their needs and resources, it never assumed that they were the only ones to make inappropriate choices. Thus in 1975, the Group established the nucleus of a unit, Appropriate Technology in the United Kingdom (AT/UK), to provide a stimulus and a focus for local organisations interested in the advancement of small enterprises and of the technologies appropriate to such enterprises. In Britain, the decline of the manufacturing industries and, in particular, of the small firms sector is now the subject of widespread concern. There is the growing realisation that large organisations are often overmanned and are unable to utilise fully the resources of men and machinery available to them, such that plans to encourage greater investment do not seem likely to generate significant employment in the large firm sectors. [23] Working with a network of Local Enterprise Trusts, AT/UK has already been successful in stimulating the creation of several hundred new employment opportunities in the small enterprise sector and helped to show that the "Small is Beautiful" philosophy is not stamped "For Export Only".

POLICY CONSIDERATIONS AND PRIORITIES

The foregoing analysis suggests a number of priority areas in which further assistance should be concentrated.

Policies, Dissemination and Implementation

1. National technology policies and plans: Many developing countries are formulating national technology policies and plan aimed at encouraging the use of appropriate technologies and promoting the small industry sector, particularly in rural areas. Although a wide variety of measures have been tried, there has been little objective research to evaluate their relative merits and so help policy-makers to make a reasonably accurate prediction of the benefits (and costs) of introducing specific legislation and administrative measures in a specific socio-economic environment. Yet the indifferent results that are likely to accrue from such a haphazard approach could easily bring such policies into disrepute. Thus there is a good case for a systematic evaluation of case studies covering the spectrum of available policy measures in a range of countries. The results of this research will need to be disseminated by making available specialist expertise to review current policies and propose improvements in accordance with the lessons learned from the research applied to local parameters.

2. Support to national Appropriate Technology Centres: The staff of AT Centres are the frontline troops in the battle to disseminate knowledge of appropriate technologies and ensure that AT projects yield the maximum possible benefit for village people. AT Centres are essentially contact organisations and form a crucial link between the special needs and conditions of individual rural communities and the resources and skills available from external research, development and knowledge organisations. AT Centres can only be effective if their staffs are sensitive to the (often subtle) variations in social economic and cultural standards that must be understood if problems are to be diagnosed and treated appropriately. It is this need to be fully attuned to local conditions that makes national AT centres a much more promising proposition than regional centres. Inevitably such centres usually start with a small core of professional staff, so external assistance is necessary to provide the impetus to define and implement specific projects and programmes. The response must be both flexible and prompt, as the input of specialist assistance on a short term consultancy basis is usually more supportive than the more cumbersome and costly long term secondment of technical experts whose expertise may prove less well-suited to the centres' evolving needs.

3. Communication between national AT Centres: There is little that outside agencies can do to assist AT centres in forging links with the communities that they are set up to serve. But assistance can be given in other linkages – both with outside resources and with other AT centres which may be facing – and solving – parallel problems. The links will prove more resilient if they are flexible, and the sort of 'knowledge of knowledge service that ITDG seeks to provide is very relevant.

4. Small business promotion: The small enterprise sector is the "silent partner" of the AT movement, since small businesses create the most jobs per unit of invested capital, and show the highest outputs per unit of capital and per unit of energy consumed. They also tend to spread wealth more evenly in a community than do large investment projects in which only the wealthy can participate. An example of the growing significance of the sector in the strategy of international agencies is the rapid growth of World Bank lending to small business from 6 per cent of its business lending in 1976, to 24 per cent currently, and by 1981 it should touch 30 per cent.[24] Inadequate managerial capacity is often a more serious constraint on small enterprise performance than is a pure shortage of funds, and there is immense scope for all agencies to contribute to the major advisory and training effort that is called for.

Education and Training

1. Training for Appropriate Technological choice: Once an inappropriate technology has been chosen and installed, the costs of remedying the error become disproportionate. Hence the importance of improving the quality of professional performance in making the initial choice. The selection of the appropriate technology in any given instance is – providing it is properly done – by no means a routine matter of comparing a few figures on a sheet of paper. Decision makers need to be aware of the full range of possible options as well as being sensitive to the impact that each would make on the local community and its environment. The initiative of the ILO in commencing research in this area has been noted, but there is a role for other agencies in planning and implementing training courses for those who will be involved in helping local people come to the right decision on the technology that would be appropriate in their own special circumstances.

2. Attention to training curricula: General training and educational curricula should be formulated to match national policies for the promotion of appropriate technology. However, too often these curricula subvert AT-oriented policies due to an unnoticed bias towards sophisticated technologies which is implicit in capital-intensive- compatible courses. A crucial priority is in expansion in supervisory training, since a lack of competent supervisors is often the key constraint which causes governments to avoid the employment opportunities that could be achieved if they were to adopt labour-based technologies. It is important that the majority of students in technical colleges and universities, especially engineers and economists, should be taught about the concept of appropriate technology and the major role it can play in development. If such teaching is to be undertaken, course material will have to be prepared and lecturers found who are competent to present it; possibly specialist personnel who might run short courses or give a series of lectures.[25]

3. AT training - Professional level: There is a need to arrange for the communication of AT concepts and practical techniques to the designers and operating staff of institutions and enterprises engaged on general development programmes and projects in developing countries. The design stage is vital on most projects, since it is at this stage that technologies are chosen (and frozen), funds are effectively committed and the possibility of ensuring that the project is truly appropriate is either grasped or lost. Yet too often the designer is remote from the eventual project site and has only a sketchy idea of the desires and needs of the people who will (hopefully) benefit from the project he is planning.

4. AT training - Artisan level: The limited needs of artisans who will be working on AT projects are not really catered for in the conventional examination-oriented trades courses that are at present run in most trade schools and technical colleges. Instead they require a basic general knowledge of a wide range of skills rather than an in-depth treatment of a particular trade.

5. AT training - Supervisory and Managerial level: A shortage of 'front-line' managers' is often the critical constraint on the adoption of labour-based technologies since they can only be economically justified if the operators achieve acceptable levels of productivity. Thus practical training in planning, supervision, record-keeping, control and simple man-management techniques could make AT a much more practical proposition by raising levels of output to a competitive level.

REFERENCES

1. Drucker, P.F. **Technology, Management and Society** Heinemann, London 1970.

2. Ministry of Overseas Development. **Appropriate Technology** Overseas Development Paper No. 8. HMSO, London 1977.

3. Jequier, N. **Appropriate Technology: Problems and Promises** OECD, Paris 1976.

4. **Training Managers for Appropriate Technological Choice** (Draft – unpublished). ILO, Geneva 1979.

5. Schumacher, E.F. **Small is Beautiful: a study of economics as if people mattered.** Blond & Briggs, 1973.

6. McRobie, G. **Technology for Development – Small is Beautiful.** Journal of the Royal Society of Arts, March 1974.

7. United Nations. **World Economic Survey.** United Nations, New York 1965.

8. Frost, D.H. **Appropriate Industrial Technology: An Integrated Approach.** Paper to the International Forum on Appropriate Industrial Technology. ITDG, London June, 1978.

9. McRobie, G and Parry, J.P.M. **'Report on the Promotion of Small-Scale Industries in the Rural Areas of Tanzania'** ITDG

10. Pakistan Appropriate Technology Development Organisation '5th and 6th Combined Bi-annual Reports – July '76 – June '77.' ATPO, Pakistan July, 1977.

11. Jequier, N. **Appropriate Technology: Some Criteria** in Bhalla, A.S. "Towards Global Action for Appropriate Technology", Pergamon, Oxford 1979.

12. ITDG Annual Report and Accounts – 1974.

13. **Science and Technology for Development.** British National Paper for the United Nations Conference on Science and Technology for Development, 1979.

14. Holtermann S. **Intermediate Technology in Ghana: The Experience of Kumasi University's Technology Consultancy Centre.** Intermediate Technology Industrial Services, Rugby, UK 1979.

15. **Report of the UNIDO Regional Workshop on the Use of Consultants – Tokyo, Japan, 1 – 13 December, 1969.** United Nations, New York, 1970.

16. **Management Consulting: A Guide to the Profession.** ILO, Geneva 1976.

17. Seers, D. and Joy, L. **Development in a Divided World.** Penguin Books, London 1971.

18. Harper, M. 'Appropriate Consultancy for Small Business'. **Appropriate Technology**: Vol. 2 No. 1, May 1975.

19. Harper, Malcolm. **Consultancy for Small Business.** IT Publications Ltd., London 1977.

20. Miles, Derek. **Accounting and Book-keeping for the Small Building Contractor.** IT Publications Ltd., London 1978.

21. Miles, Derek. **Financial Planning for the Small Building Contractor.** IT Publications Ltd., London 1979.

22. Miles, Derek. **The Small Building Contractor and the Client.** IT Publications Ltd., London 1980.

23. Davis, John. **Technology for a Changing World.** IT Publications Ltd., London 1978.

24. Thackray, J. **Small US Business Gets Big.** Management Today. January 1980.

25. Appropriate Technology for Small-Scale Industries: Possible Roles for Development Finance Institutions in Africa. ECA Ref. E/CN.14/INR/219. May 1977.

www.ingramcontent.com/pod-product-compliance
Ingram Content Group UK Ltd.
Pitfield, Milton Keynes, MK11 3LW, UK
UKHW060844160426
5217IPUK00042B/2085